The Passion Path Journal

Create a Joyful Life Through Daily Reflections and Action

Karen Putz

Copyright © 2019 Barefoot Publications

All rights reserved. No part of this publication may be reproduced, stored in a retrieval system, or transmitted in any form or by any means – electronic, mechanical, photocopy, recording, scanning, or other-except for brief quotations in critical reviews or articles, without the prior written permission of the publisher.

This book is available for quantity discounts for bulk purchases.

For additional information about Karen Putz at Ageless Passions or The Passion School, visit www.agelesspassions.com
or email:
Karen@agelesspassions.com

DEDICATION

This journal is dedicated to YOU.

Unwrap the gift of passion.

Pursue your passion and everything else will fall into place. This is not being romantic. This is the highest order of pragmatism."

~Gabby Giffords

"Passion is your joy. It is the essence of who you are. You have to unwrap it to find it. Passion is like tap water—turn it on and it flows. The mind, body, and soul become one when you tap into your passion."

~Jackie St. Onge

INTRODUCTION

The Passion Path

Passion is unique to you.

You, and only you, can know, define, and understand what passion means to you.

Passion has clues, but many times we become so busy with life that we miss the opportunities that show up in our life. This journal is your opportunity to look within. Seek first to understand—then to go forth and live.

The Passion Path Journal is your own personal journey down the passion path that is right for you. By knowing and understanding what is deep in your soul and focusing daily energy toward your joy—you can then create the life you truly want to live.

Why the Passion Path Journal?

There is power in the written word. Writing out your thoughts is an ancient art. For thousands of years, humans have been recording their thoughts, ideas, and creativity. Your written words become the map and GPS system that helps guide you on the Passion Path.

This journal is designed to help you create a daily ritual that keeps you focused on what really matters to you: to live YOUR passion.

Journaling is part of the Passion Path that you implement daily.

How to Use this Journal

There are three daily activities as part of the Passion Path.

Part I:
Each day has a different question for you to ponder. Write freely. There is power that comes from letting the thoughts flow on paper. Write from the heart. Allow yourself to go deep with your answers without censoring what you are thinking/feeling/writing.

Part II:
Plan for three action items in your day. Remember this: every decision and action that you take each day is either aligned with meaningful purpose or dragging you further away from the life you truly want.

Part III:

At the end of each day, reflect with gratitude on the moments throughout your day that brought you joy, bliss, and happiness. What you focus on, expands. This practice of gratitude reflection brings a positive energy into your life. It is difficult to dwell on negative feelings when you are focused on what is *good* in your life.

The Impact of a Daily Ritual

It's all too easy to begin a new habit and then allow it to fall to the wayside after a few days. When you put a new ritual in place, you must get into a rhythm of repetition to be able to implement the powerful effects.

When you focus on what brings you joy and take daily action in meaningful ways, *and* then reflect in gratitude each day—you will live life in a whole new way.

Here's to YOUR passion!

> "It's your place in the world; it's your life. Go on and do all you can with it, and make it the life you want to live."
>
> ~Mae Jemison

The Passion Path Journal

"Knowing yourself is the beginning of all wisdom."

~Aristotle

Who Am I?

_____
_____
_____
_____
_____
_____
_____
_____
_____
_____
_____
_____
_____
_____

Today's Passion Plan:

1. _____

2. _____

3. _____

Today's Passion Gratitude:

1. _____

2. _____

3. _____

> "Sometimes you have to take a step back to go forward."
>
> ~Marianne Renner

Looking back in the past, what were my moments of joy?

_____
_____
_____
_____
_____
_____
_____
_____
_____
_____
_____
_____
_____
_____

Today's Passion Plan:

1. _____

2. _____

3. _____

Today's Passion Gratitude:

1. _____

2. _____

3. _____

"Something opens our wings."

~Rumi

The Present: Where does my mind wander to when I'm not engaged in an activity?

___
___
___
___
___
___
___
___
___
___
___
___

Today's Passion Plan:

1. _____

2. _____

3. _____

Today's Passion Gratitude:

1. _____

2. _____

3. _____

> *"The scariest thought in the world is that someday I'll wake up and realize I've been sleepwalking through life."*
>
> ~George Saunders

The Future: What's on my "Someday List?"

_____
_____
_____
_____
_____
_____
_____
_____
_____
_____
_____
_____
_____
_____
_____
_____

Today's Passion Plan:

1. _____

2. _____

3. _____

Today's Passion Gratitude:

1. _____

2. _____

3. _____

> "I decided to fly through the air and live in the sunlight and enjoy life as much as I could."
>
> ~Evel Knievel

When my life is ideal, I am:

_____
_____
_____
_____
_____
_____
_____
_____
_____
_____
_____
_____

Today's Passion Plan:

1. _____

2. _____

3. _____

Today's Passion Gratitude:

1. _____

2. _____

3. _____

> "To me, every hour of the day and night is an unspeakably perfect miracle."
>
> ~Walter Chrysler

What does the "perfect" day look like?

_____
_____
_____
_____
_____
_____
_____
_____
_____
_____
_____
_____
_____
_____

Today's Passion Plan:

1. _____

2. _____

3. _____

Today's Passion Gratitude:

1. _____

2. _____

3. _____

> "Do what you love, and you will find the way to get it out to the world."
>
> ~Judy Collins

What do I wish I could do?

_____

_____
_____
_____
_____
_____
_____
_____
_____
_____
_____
_____

Today's Passion Plan:

1. _____

2. _____

3. _____

Today's Passion Gratitude:

1. _____

2. _____

3. _____

> "If you do what you love, you'll never work a day in your life."
>
> ~Marc Anthony

What do I love about my life?

_____
_____
_____
_____
_____
_____
_____
_____
_____
_____
_____
_____
_____
_____

Today's Passion Plan:

1. _____

2. _____

3. _____

Today's Passion Gratitude:

1. _____

2. _____

3. _____

> "We experience happiness as a series of pleasing moments."
>
> ~Tara Stiles

What is an "Awe" moment that I remember fondly?

_____
_____
_____
_____
_____
_____
_____
_____
_____
_____
_____
_____

Today's Passion Plan:

1. _____

2. _____

3. _____

Today's Passion Gratitude:

1. _____

2. _____

3. _____

> "Anyone who has been successful and has knowledge to share is a mentor."

~Ory Okolloh

Who do I admire greatly and why?

_____
_____
_____
_____
_____
_____
_____
_____
_____
_____
_____
_____
_____

Today's Passion Plan:

1. _____

2. _____

3. _____

Today's Passion Gratitude:

1. _____

2. _____

3. _____

> "Once we believe in ourselves, we can risk curiosity, wonder, spontaneous delight, or any experience that reveals the human spirit."
>
> ~e.e. cummings

What do I want to learn more about?

_____
_____
_____
_____
_____
_____
_____
_____
_____
_____
_____
_____
_____

Today's Passion Plan:

1. _____

2. _____

3. _____

Today's Passion Gratitude:

1. _____

2. _____

3. _____

> "Develop a passion for learning. If you do, you will never cease to grow."
>
> ~Anthony D'Angelo

What was my favorite class in school and why?

_____
_____
_____
_____
_____
_____
_____
_____
_____
_____
_____

Today's Passion Plan:

1. _____

2. _____

3. _____

Today's Passion Gratitude:

1. _____

2. _____

3. _____

> "The most beautiful things are not associated with money; they are memories and moments. If you don't celebrate those, they can pass you by."
>
> ~Alek Wek

What's working well in my life?

_____
_____
_____
_____
_____
_____
_____
_____
_____
_____

Today's Passion Plan:

1. _____

2. _____

3. _____

Today's Passion Gratitude:

1. _____

2. _____

3. _____

> "Cherish your visions and your dreams as they are the children of your soul, the blueprints of your ultimate achievements."
>
> ~Napoleon Hill

What do I dream of?

_____
_____
_____
_____
_____
_____
_____
_____
_____
_____
_____
_____
_____

Today's Passion Plan:

1. _____

2. _____

3. _____

Today's Passion Gratitude:

1. _____

2. _____

3. _____

"For each one of us stands alone in the midst of a universe."

~John Buchanan Robinson

What do I stand for?

_____
_____
_____
_____
_____
_____
_____
_____
_____
_____
_____

Today's Passion Plan:

1. _____

2. _____

3. _____

Today's Passion Gratitude:

1. _____

2. _____

3. _____

> "Only I can change my life. No one can do it for me."
>
> ~Carol Burnett

What can I change right now?

_____
_____
_____
_____
_____
_____
_____
_____
_____
_____
_____
_____
_____

Today's Passion Plan:

1. _____

2. _____

3. _____

Today's Passion Gratitude:

1. _____

2. _____

3. _____

> "Your success and happiness lies in you. Resolve to keep happy, and your joy and you shall form an invincible host against difficulties."
>
> ~Helen Keller

What brings me joy?

_____
_____
_____
_____
_____
_____
_____
_____
_____
_____
_____
_____
_____

Today's Passion Plan:

1. _____

2. _____

3. _____

Today's Passion Gratitude:

1. _____

2. _____

3. _____

> "I surround myself with good people who make me feel great and give me positive energy."
>
> ~Ali Krieger

Who do I want to spend more time with?

_____
_____
_____
_____
_____
_____
_____
_____
_____
_____

Today's Passion Plan:

1. _____

2. _____

3. _____

Today's Passion Gratitude:

1. _____

2. _____

3. _____

> "When a person talks about their dreams, something bubbles up from within. Their eyes brighten, their face glows, and you can feel the excitement in their words."
>
> ~John Maxwell

What am I excited about?

___
___
___
___
___
___
___
___
___
___
___
___

Today's Passion Plan:

1. _____

2. _____

3. _____

Today's Passion Gratitude:

1. _____

2. _____

3. _____

"Follow your heart, and the mind will follow you. Believe in yourself, and you will create miracles."

~Kailash Satyarthi

What do I believe?

Today's Passion Plan:

1. _____

2. _____

3. _____

Today's Passion Gratitude:

1. _____

2. _____

3. _____

> "The mediocre teacher tells. The good teacher explains. The superior teacher demonstrates. The great teacher inspires."
>
> ~William Arthur Ward

Who was my favorite teacher in life?

Today's Passion Plan:

1. _____

2. _____

3. _____

Today's Passion Gratitude:

1. _____

2. _____

3. _____

> "Follow your bliss and the universe will open doors where there were only walls."
>
> ~Joseph Campbell

What brings bliss into my life?

_____

_____

_____

_____

_____

_____

_____

_____

_____

_____

_____

_____

_____

Today's Passion Plan:

1. _____

2. _____

3. _____

Today's Passion Gratitude:

4. _____

5. _____

6. _____

> "It's not enough to have lived. We should be determined to live for something."
>
> ~Winston Churchill

What matters most to me?

_____
_____
_____
_____
_____
_____
_____
_____
_____
_____
_____
_____
_____

Today's Passion Plan:

1. _____

2. _____

3. _____

Today's Passion Gratitude:

1. _____

2. _____

3. _____

> "Here's the truth: we absolutely get to choose our path."
>
> ~Bob Doyle

What is life about?

_____
_____
_____
_____
_____
_____
_____
_____
_____
_____
_____
_____
_____

Today's Passion Plan:

1. _____

2. _____

3. _____

Today's Passion Gratitude:

1. _____

2. _____

3. _____

> "When I stand before God at the end of my life, I would hope that I would not have a single bit of talent left and could say, 'I used everything you gave me.'"
>
> ~Erma Bombeck

If I arrived at the end of my life today, what would I regret?

_____

_____
_____
_____
_____
_____
_____
_____
_____
_____
_____
_____

Today's Passion Plan:

1. _____

2. _____

3. _____

Today's Passion Gratitude:

1. _____

2. _____

3. _____

"Enjoy the journey and try to get better every day. And don't lose the passion and the love for what you do."

~Nadia Comaneci

What's the best thing about my life?

Today's Passion Plan:

1. _____

2. _____

3. _____

Today's Passion Gratitude:

1. _____

2. _____

3. _____

"Find a reason to laugh each day. It's the little things in life that make you happy."

~Faith Hill

What makes me laugh?

Today's Passion Plan:

1. _____

2. _____

3. _____

Today's Passion Gratitude:

1. _____

2. _____

3. _____

> "Focus on the journey, not the destination. The doing is often more important than the outcome."
>
> ~Greg Anderson

If my life continued on the same path years from now, would that be okay?

_____
_____
_____
_____
_____
_____
_____
_____
_____
_____
_____
_____
_____

Today's Passion Plan:

1. _____

2. _____

3. _____

Today's Passion Gratitude:

1. _____

2. _____

3. _____

> "There is no passion to be found playing small, in settling for a life that is less than the one you are capable of living."
>
> ~Nelson Mandela

What are some ways I am "playing small" with my life?

_____
_____
_____
_____
_____
_____
_____
_____
_____
_____
_____
_____

Today's Passion Plan:

1. _____

2. _____

3. _____

Today's Passion Gratitude:

1. _____

2. _____

3. _____

> "The things you are passionate about are not random, they are your calling."
>
> ~Fabienne Fredrickson

When I was a little kid, what did I want to be?

_____

_____
_____
_____
_____
_____
_____
_____
_____
_____
_____

Today's Passion Plan:

1. _____

2. _____

3. _____

Today's Passion Gratitude:

1. _____

2. _____

3. _____

> "A true passion that burns within your soul
> is one that can never be put out."
>
> ~Zach Toelke

That little voice inside of me, what does it say?

_____
_____
_____
_____
_____
_____
_____
_____
_____
_____
_____
_____

Today's Passion Plan:

1. _____

2. _____

3. _____

Today's Passion Gratitude:

1. _____

2. _____

3. _____

> "If you feel like there's something out there that you're supposed to be doing, if you have a passion for it, then stop wishing and just do it."
>
> ~Wanda Sykes

What do I think I'm "supposed to be doing?"

_____
_____
_____
_____
_____
_____
_____
_____
_____
_____
_____

Today's Passion Plan:

1. _____

2. _____

3. _____

Today's Passion Gratitude:

1. _____

2. _____

3. _____

> "Nothing is as important as passion. No matter what you want to do with your life, be passionate."
>
> ~Jon Bon Jovi

What holds me back in life?

_____
_____
_____
_____
_____
_____
_____
_____
_____
_____
_____
_____

Today's Passion Plan:

1. _____

2. _____

3. _____

Today's Passion Gratitude:

1. _____

2. _____

3. _____

> "Your work is to discover your work and then with all your heart to give yourself to it."
>
> ~Buddha

What is my purpose?

_____
_____
_____
_____
_____
_____
_____
_____
_____
_____

Today's Passion Plan:

1. _____

2. _____

3. _____

Today's Passion Gratitude:

1. _____

2. _____

3. _____

> "Be fearless in the pursuit of what sets your soul on fire."
>
> ~Unknown

What sets my soul on fire?

_____
_____
_____
_____
_____
_____
_____
_____
_____
_____
_____
_____
_____

Today's Passion Plan:

1. _____

2. _____

3. _____

Today's Passion Gratitude:

1. _____

2. _____

3. _____

> "Passion isn't something that lives way up in the sky in abstract dreams and hopes. It lives at ground level, in the specific details of what you're actually doing every day."

~Marcus Buckingham

What fears are holding me back?

_____
_____
_____
_____
_____
_____
_____
_____
_____
_____
_____
_____
_____

Today's Passion Plan:

1. _____

2. _____

3. _____

Today's Passion Gratitude:

1. _____

2. _____

3. _____

"Follow your passion. Nothing—not wealth, success, accolades, or fame—is worth spending a lifetime doing things you don't enjoy."

~Jonathan Sacks

What do I enjoy doing most?

Today's Passion Plan:

1. _____

2. _____

3. _____

Today's Passion Gratitude:

1. _____

2. _____

3. _____

> "Passion and purpose go hand in hand. When you discover your purpose, you will normally find it's something you're tremendously passionate about."
>
> ~Steve Pavlina

What activities bore me?

_____
_____
_____
_____
_____
_____
_____
_____
_____
_____
_____
_____

Today's Passion Plan:

1. _____

2. _____

3. _____

Today's Passion Gratitude:

1. _____

2. _____

3. _____

"Too many of us are not living our dreams because we are living our fears."

~Les Brown

What scares me the most about life?

Today's Passion Plan:

1. _____

2. _____

3. _____

Today's Passion Gratitude:

1. _____

2. _____

3. _____

"If you're passionate about what you do, then you're doing to be looking for everything you can to get better at it."

~Jack Canfield

What am I passionate about?

Today's Passion Plan:

1. _____

2. _____

3. _____

Today's Passion Gratitude:

1. _____

2. _____

3. _____

> "Everyone has talent. What's rare is the courage to follow it to the dark places where it leads."
>
> ~Erica Jong

What is my greatest ability?

Today's Passion Plan:

1. _____

2. _____

3. _____

Today's Passion Gratitude:

1. _____

2. _____

3. _____

> "Always follow your passion no matter what, because even if it's not the same financial success, it'll lead you to the money that'll make you the happiest."
>
> ~Ellen DeGeneres

What makes me happy?

_____
_____
_____
_____
_____
_____
_____
_____
_____
_____
_____
_____

Today's Passion Plan:

1. _____

2. _____

3. _____

Today's Passion Gratitude:

1. _____

2. _____

3. _____

"When you have a passion for something, then you tend not only to be better at it, but you work hard at it too."

~Vera Wang

What am I willing to work hard for?

Today's Passion Plan:

1. _____

2. _____

3. _____

Today's Passion Gratitude:

1. _____

2. _____

3. _____

> "I would rather die of passion than of boredom."
>
> ~Vincent Van Gogh

What energizes me?

_____
_____
_____
_____
_____
_____
_____
_____
_____
_____
_____
_____
_____
_____
_____

Today's Passion Plan:

1. _____

2. _____

3. _____

Today's Passion Gratitude:

1. _____

2. _____

3. _____

> "Worry never robs tomorrow of its sorrow,
> it only saps today of its joy."
>
> ~Leo Buscaglia

What keeps me up worrying at night?

_____
_____
_____
_____
_____
_____
_____
_____
_____
_____
_____
_____
_____

Today's Passion Plan:

1. _____

2. _____

3. _____

Today's Passion Gratitude:

1. _____

2. _____

3. _____

> "He who has a why to live for can bear almost any how."
>
> ~Friedrich Nietzsche

What is my "Why?"

_____
_____
_____
_____
_____
_____
_____
_____
_____
_____
_____
_____
_____
_____

Today's Passion Plan:

1. _____

2. _____

3. _____

Today's Passion Gratitude:

1. _____

2. _____

3. _____

> "It doesn't interest me what you do for a living. I want to know what you ache for, and if you dream of meeting your heart's longing."
>
> ~Oriah

What do I long for?

Today's Passion Plan:

1. _____

2. _____

3. _____

Today's Passion Gratitude:

1. _____

2. _____

3. _____

> "It's never too late to be what you might have been."
>
> ~George Eliot

What do I wish I could do?

Today's Passion Plan:

1. _____

2. _____

3. _____

Today's Passion Gratitude:

1. _____

2. _____

3. _____

> "The aim of life is self-development, to realize one's nature perfectly."
>
> ~Oscar Wilde

What do I want to change?

_____
_____
_____
_____
_____
_____
_____
_____
_____
_____
_____
_____
_____
_____

Today's Passion Plan:

1. _____

2. _____

3. _____

Today's Passion Gratitude:

1. _____

2. _____

3. _____

"When you are grateful—when you can see what you have—you unlock blessings to flow in your life."

~Suze Orman

What activities put me in a state of "flow?"

Today's Passion Plan:

1. _____

2. _____

3. _____

Today's Passion Gratitude:

1. _____

2. _____

3. _____

"The most important skill you need is the ability to learn how to change and grow."

~Scott Cook

What skills come to me easily?

Today's Passion Plan:

1. _____

2. _____

3. _____

Today's Passion Gratitude:

1. _____

2. _____

3. _____

"The presence of passion within you is the greatest gift you can receive. Treat it as a miracle."

~Wayne Dyer

What do I pray/wish for?

Today's Passion Plan:

1. _____

2. _____

3. _____

Today's Passion Gratitude:

1. _____

2. _____

3. _____

> "Dream lofty dreams, and as you dream, so you shall become."
>
> ~James Allen

What's my BIG dream?

Today's Passion Plan:

1. _____

2. _____

3. _____

Today's Passion Gratitude:

1. _____

2. _____

3. _____

> "The only advice I can offer is to find what you love to do, find the joy in it, and express yourself through your passion."
>
> ~Barry Williams

How do I want to be remembered?

_____

_____

_____

_____

_____

_____

_____

_____

_____

_____

_____

Today's Passion Plan:

1. _____

2. _____

3. _____

Today's Passion Gratitude:

1. _____

2. _____

3. _____

> "Life is a great big canvas and you should throw all the paint on it you can."
>
> ~Danny Kaye

HOW do I want to live?

_____
_____
_____
_____
_____
_____
_____
_____
_____
_____
_____

Today's Passion Plan:

4. _____

5. _____

6. _____

Today's Passion Gratitude:

4. _____

5. _____

6. _____

The Passion Path Journal

CLOSING THOUGHTS

By now, you are well on your Passion Path if you've completed your journal and reached this page.

Clarity comes from taking action on what's in your heart and putting it into your life. You are among the 13% who have chosen to focus on a process that brings clarity to the Passion Path.

I'd love to hear about your Passion Path journey. What did you learn from this process? Email me at karen@agelesspassions.com with "Passion Path" in the subject line and share your wins.

Here's to YOUR passion!

Love,
Karen

"You can see yourself as a wave in the ocean or you can see yourself as the ocean."

~Oprah Winfrey

ABOUT THE AUTHOR

Karen Putz is known as "The Passion Mentor." She is the author of several books, including "Unwrapping Your Passion, Creating the Life You Truly Want." She is a certified Passion Test Facilitator. Karen's background is Counseling (B.S.) and Rehabilitation Counseling (M.A.) and she provides Passion Coaching services.

To learn more about how you can unwrap your passion and live YOUR passion, visit The Passion School:

www.thepassionschool.com

Made in United States
Troutdale, OR
01/10/2024